CATS SET I

MANX CATS

Tamara L. Britton
ABDO Publishing Company

visit us at
www.abdopublishing.com

Published by ABDO Publishing Company, 8000 West 78th Street, Edina, Minnesota 55439. Copyright © 2011 by Abdo Consulting Group, Inc. International copyrights reserved in all countries. No part of this book may be reproduced in any form without written permission from the publisher. The Checkerboard Library™ is a trademark and logo of ABDO Publishing Company.

Printed in the United States of America, North Mankato, Minnesota.
042010
092010

 PRINTED ON RECYCLED PAPER

Cover Photo: Photo by Helmi Flick
Interior Photos: Alamy p. 12; Corbis pp. 9, 21;
    Photo by Helmi Flick pp. 5, 7, 10, 11, 13, 19; Peter Arnold p. 17; Photolibrary p. 14

Editor: Megan M. Gunderson
Art Direction & Cover Design: Neil Klinepier

Library of Congress Cataloging-in-Publication Data

Britton, Tamara L., 1963-
  Manx cats / Tamara L. Britton.
      p. cm. -- (Cats)
  Includes index.
  ISBN 978-1-61613-399-3
  1. Manx cat--Juvenile literature. I. Title.
  SF449.M36B75 2011
  636.8'22--dc22
                                        2010014952

CONTENTS

Lions, Tigers, and Cats 4

Manx Cats 6

Qualities 8

Coat and Color 10

Size 12

Care 14

Feeding 16

Kittens 18

Buying a Kitten 20

Glossary 22

Web Sites 23

Index 24

LIONS, TIGERS, AND CATS

Domestic cats have a long history. Their ancestors are African wildcats. About 3,500 years ago, ancient Egyptians began to tame these cats. The cats kept rats and mice out of grain the Egyptians had stored.

Soon, others began to see the benefits of these helpful creatures. People in Europe and North and South America began keeping cats, too. Today, there are more than 40 different **breeds** of domestic cats.

All these cats are members of the family **Felidae**. There are 37 species in this family. Other members of this family are lions and tigers!

The Manx cat

MANX CATS

The Manx cat got its start hundreds of years ago on the Isle of Man. This island nation lies in the Irish Sea. It sits between the islands of Great Britain and Ireland.

As the Isle of Man is an island, many ships docked there. Cats that arrived on the ships went ashore. There, they mated with local **domestic** cats. At some point in time, a mutation occurred in the cats. This change caused kittens to be born without tails!

The tailless cats became common on the Isle of Man. These unusual cats charmed travelers there. Visitors began to take the cats back to their home countries.

In the United States, the **Cat Fanciers' Association (CFA)** recognized the Manx cat in the 1920s. Long-haired Manx were recognized in 1994.

Long-haired Manx were first recognized in 1989 as a separate breed called the Cymric.

QUALITIES

Manx cats are affectionate and loyal. They make sweet, loving pets. These even-tempered cats get along well with kids and dogs. However, Manx also enjoy quiet, relaxed surroundings.

Many people call the Manx the "dog cat." These cats have many doglike qualities. They can be taught to fetch toys and will sometimes even bury them! The cats can also be protective of their homes.

Manx cats are generally quiet cats. When they do speak up, they have a soft voice. But they will not hesitate to give an opinion when necessary!

Manx are naturally curious and like to explore. They are also powerful jumpers! You may need to put delicate items out of reach.

COAT AND COLOR

The Manx cat can have a short or long coat. Both are double coats. The short coat has an outer layer of longer, glossy hairs. These cover a short, cottony undercoat.

Long coats are dense, soft and silky, and medium length. The hair on the back end, neck, and underside is longer. Tufts of hair stick out from the ears and between the toes.

Different-colored eyes stand out against a solid white coat!

10

Manx cats can be any color or pattern. There are solid, smoke, **tabby**, and **bicolored** Manx. The Manx cat's eye color depends on the color of its coat. It can have copper, green, hazel, or blue eyes. Sometimes, each eye is a different color!

An orange tabby coat is common for a Manx cat.

SIZE

Manx are medium-sized cats. Males weigh 10 to 12 pounds (4.5 to 5.5 kg). Females are smaller. They range from 8 to 10 pounds (3.5 to 4.5 kg).

The Manx has a broad, round head on a short, thick neck. Its round **muzzle** sits between prominent cheeks. The large, round eyes are slightly angled at the outside. So, they tilt up toward the ears. The cat's ears are wide at the base and taper to rounded tips.

Manx have solid, well-muscled bodies. These sturdy cats

A rumpy riser

A rumpy

have broad chests. The short back leads to the rounded rear end. There, you can see the feature that makes Manx cats special.

Many Manx cats have no tail! There is a slight dimple where the tail should be. These Manx are called rumpies. Manx with fewer than four tail **vertebrae** are known as rumpy risers. Those with short tails are called stumpies. Manx with regular tails are called longies.

Short, heavy legs support the Manx's stout body. The rear legs are longer than the front legs. This makes the rump higher than the shoulders. All this feline fabulousness stands on rounded paws.

CARE

Cats are naturally clean animals. They use their rough tongues to groom their coats. Because of this, cats can swallow a lot of hair. So, brush your Manx once a week. Regular brushing will prevent hairballs from forming in the cat's stomach.

This longy is resting in the garden. However, Manx cats that stay indoors have less risk of injury.

A cat's natural cleanliness includes an instinct to bury its waste. So, you can train your Manx to use a **litter box**. Keep the box in a quiet place away from the cat's food and water. And, be sure to remove waste from the box daily.

Cats naturally hunt outdoors. There, they sharpen their claws on trees. Indoor cats need a scratching post. This allows them to sharpen their claws without damaging furniture or carpet.

Manx cats are very playful. Toys such as a ball or a catnip mouse are a great source of entertainment.

Manx cats are solid, healthy cats. Still, it is important to develop a relationship with a veterinarian. The veterinarian can provide yearly checkups and **vaccines**. He or she can also **spay** or **neuter** your cat.

FEEDING

When you adopt your Manx, keep feeding it the same diet it ate before. If you want to change food, slowly mix the new food with the old. This will prevent your cat from getting an upset stomach.

Cats are carnivores. They need meat in their diets! You must feed your Manx cat food that contains beef, poultry, or fish. A good commercial food will provide this and other **nutrients** your cat needs.

There are three kinds of commercial cat food. They are dry, semimoist, and canned. The food label will tell you how much and how often to feed your cat. Serve the food in a clean bowl. Also provide a bowl of fresh, clean water.

Some indoor cats tend to put on weight. If your cat's weight concerns you, check with your veterinarian about its feeding schedule.

Some cats enjoy an occasional commercial cat treat or a spot of milk!

KITTENS

Manx cats can reproduce once they are 7 to 12 months old. The female is **pregnant** for 63 to 65 days. She may have three **litters** each year. There will be about three to five kittens in each litter. A single litter can include rumpies, rumpy risers, stumpies, and longies!

At birth, Manx kittens are blind and deaf. When they are two weeks old, they begin to see and hear. Manx kittens begin to play and explore within their first three weeks. By then, their sight and hearing have improved. Their teeth are also coming in.

Manx kittens stay with their **breeder** longer than other kittens. This breed is healthy overall. But, some kittens are born with Manx Syndrome. This is a flaw in the kitten's spine.

Only rumpy and rumpy riser Manx can enter championship competitions at CFA shows.

The **breeder** will know soon after the kitten's birth if it has this illness. A reputable breeder will only allow healthy Manx kittens to be adopted.

BUYING A KITTEN

Do you think you want a Manx kitten? If so, look for a good **breeder**. Manx cats can also be found at rescue organizations. Your local shelter may have Manx cats to adopt, too.

The cost of a Manx kitten depends on its tail length and **pedigree**. Rumpy kittens that come from award-winning parents may cost hundreds of dollars. If you buy a rumpy kitten, you should file its pedigree papers with the **CFA**.

When buying a kitten, check closely to make sure it is healthy. Its ears, nose, mouth, and fur should be clean. The eyes should be bright and clear. The kitten should be alert and interested in its surroundings.

Make your decision carefully! Your Manx cat will be a loving member of your family for about 15 years.

Adopting more than one kitten will provide your pets with feline playmates!

GLOSSARY

bicolored - having two colors.

breed - a group of animals sharing the same ancestors and appearance. A breeder is a person who raises animals. Raising animals is often called breeding them.

Cat Fanciers' Association (CFA) - a group that sets the standards for judging all breeds of cats.

domestic - tame, especially relating to animals.

Felidae (FEHL-uh-dee) - the scientific Latin name for the cat family. Members of this family are called felids. They include domestic cats, lions, tigers, leopards, jaguars, cougars, wildcats, lynx, and cheetahs.

litter - all of the kittens born at one time to a mother cat.

litter box - a box filled with cat litter, which is similar to sand. Cats use litter boxes to bury their waste.

muzzle - an animal's nose and jaws.

neuter (NOO-tuhr) - to remove a male animal's reproductive organs.

nutrient - a substance found in food and used in the body. It promotes growth, maintenance, and repair.

pedigree - a record of an animal's ancestors.

pregnant - having one or more babies growing within the body.

spay - to remove a female animal's reproductive organs.

tabby - a coat pattern featuring stripes or splotches of a dark color on a lighter background. Individual hairs are banded with light and dark colors.

vaccine (vak-SEEN) - a shot given to prevent illness or disease.

vertebrae (VUHR-tuh-bray) - the bones or segments of cartilage that make up the spinal column.

WEB SITES

To learn more about Manx cats, visit ABDO Publishing Company on the World Wide Web at **www.abdopublishing.com**. Web sites about Manx cats are featured on our Book Links page. These links are routinely monitored and updated to provide the most current information available.

INDEX

A

adoption 16, 19, 20, 21
Africa 4

B

body 10, 12, 13
breeder 18, 19, 20

C

care 14, 15, 16, 17
Cat Fanciers' Association 6, 20
character 8, 15, 20, 21
claws 15
coat 6, 10, 11, 14, 20
color 11

E

ears 10, 12, 20
Europe 4, 6
eyes 11, 12, 20

F

feet 10, 13
Felidae (family) 4
food 15, 16, 17

G

grooming 14

H

head 12
health 14, 15, 16, 17, 18, 19, 20
history 4, 6
hunting 15

I

Isle of Man 6

K

kittens 6, 18, 19, 20

L

legs 13
life span 21
litter box 15

M

mouth 20
muzzle 12

N

neuter 15
North America 4, 6
nose 20

R

reproduction 18

S

scratching post 15
senses 18
size 12, 13, 17
South America 4
spay 15

T

tail 6, 13, 18, 20
teeth 18
toys 8, 15

V

vaccines 15
veterinarian 15, 17

W

water 15, 16
wildcat 4